For Lisa

With thanks to Meret Meyer,
Céline Julhiet-Charvet,
Clémence Berg,
Anne de Margerie et Jean.

Published by Peter Bedrick Books
2112 Broadway, New York, NY 10023

Layout and design: Thomas Gravemaker, X-Act
All illustrations in this book are reproductions of works by Chagall.

Peter Bedrick Books and the swan logo are trademarks of Peter Bedrick Books Inc.

Printed in Mexico
5 4 3 2 1 96 97 98 99 00

Library of Congress Cataloging-in-Publication Data

Sellier, Maria
[C comme Chagall. English]
Chagall from A to Z / Marie Sellier ; translated from the French by Claudia Zoe Bedrick. — 1st American ed.
p. c.
Summary: Vignettes from the life of painter Marc Chagall are arranged under an alphabetical sequence of French words that focus on a key element of his life or work.

ISBN 0-87226-478-5
1. Chagall, Marc, 1887- —Dictionaries—Juvenile literature. 2. Artists—Russia (Federation)—Biography—Dictionaries—Juvenile literature. [1. Chagall, Marc, 1887- 2. Artists. 3. French language—Vocabulary.] I. Chagall, Marc, 1887- . II. Title.
N6999.C46S4513 1996
709' .2—dc20
[B]

96-26986
CIP
AC

Chagall from A to Z

Marie Sellier

Translated from the French by
Claudia Zoe Bedrick

PETER BEDRICK BOOKS
NEW YORK

Contents

Coqs, chévres
Chickens, Goats and Company

Dieu
God

Etoiles
Stars

Fiancée

Guerre
War

Mariés
Married

Nature

Ombre
Shadow

Pile et face
Heads or Tails

Quelques personnages
Characters

cloWn

X

Yeux
Eyes

Zone Sacrée
Sacred Space

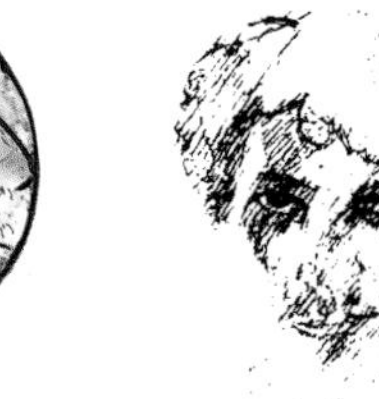

Crédits photos
Acknowledgments

Au feu!

Fire!

On July 7, 1887, in Vitebsk, Russia, the birth of a boy is celebrated. It is Zahar and Feïta-Iga's first-born. He is small and pale, in fact, too pale. His parents panic. They rub his skin and plunge him into cold water. But will he live, this baby who breathes with such difficulty? Suddenly, cries of "Fire! Fire!" ring out in the street. The small Jewish neighborhood is ablaze. The

The Birth, 1911.

Birth or cataclysm? Was Chagall thinking of his own birth when he did this painting?

wooden houses ignite like matches. It is necessary to evacuate.
The bed, with Feïta-Iga and her baby, is carried out to safety.
The baby gives a weak cry.
He will live, and they will call him Marc...Marc Chagall.

Bleu

Blue

Marc grows up in Vitebsk, a town of two rivers and two white churches. Vitebsk is blue, blending sky and water. It is blue as the Russian sky in winter, immense and icy; blue as the Dvina, the river of swirling waters; blue as Marc's dreams.

Zahar and Feïta-Iga, Marc's parents.

Feïta-Iga has great affection for her eldest son, whom she senses is different from the others, but she also has very little time to devote to him. Seven sisters and a brother have followed him into the wooden house which is similar to the other *isbas** of the Jewish

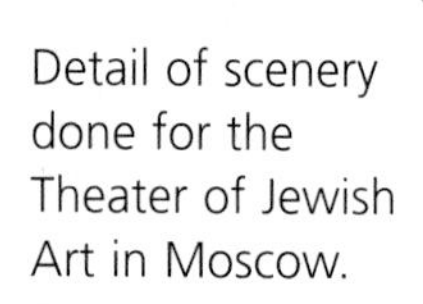

Detail of scenery done for the Theater of Jewish Art in Moscow.

A fantasy of the painter. In 1917, Marc paints this blue *isba*, behind which is a view of Vitebsk.

quarter. Between her children and her grocery store, the tiny Feïta-Iga does not rest. She has no choice. Zahar, Marc's father, is a simple worker in a herring factory.

*An *isba* is a small house, built from the wood of fir trees, specific to the countryside of northern Russia.

Coqs, chèvres

Chickens, Goats and Company

At the beginning of the century, Vitebsk is still a village. Its streets are dirt roads. When it rains, one splashes in the mud and has to take care not to be spattered by jolting carts pulled by ponies. Kitchen gardens are hidden behind wooden fences, as are backyards, the kingdom of domestic animals. There one

et compagnie

can find roosters, chickens, cows, pigs, goats, and cats, which are always ready to slip inside the house.
Marc passes his childhood amidst all of these familiar animals. Later on, he will make them his own by painting them in his own manner: roosters with tender eyes, cats with human heads, flying goats. Dogs, however, he will never paint. An old memory of a bite on his arm continues to smart. It was a bite from which he almost died.

Between painting and x-ray: *The Cattle Dealer* of 1912. Nothing escapes the painter's eye, not even the foal to be born.

Dieu

God

The Chagall family is devout. Prayer and religious festivals give life its rhythm throughout the year. Every morning at daybreak, before drinking his tea and leaving for work, Zahar goes to pray at the synagogue.

He works hard all day transporting barrels of salted herring, but he never complains. His faith in God sustains him.

Every week, the Chagalls observe the traditional rites of the Sabbath.

ehind the Jew with raditional curls, *peyas,* is he Star of David, mblem of the Jewish eligion.

1916, *The Festival of Tabernacles,* one of many Jewish festivals.

From Friday evening until sunset Saturday is a time of rest and prayer. It is also a time for getting together with the extended family of uncles and aunts and for singing and dancing to the fiddle.
Marc has begun to draw and paint, which he enjoys more than anything else in the world. He is not encouraged along this path, however, for his parents believe that the representation of the human figure is prohibited within their religion.

Etoiles

Stars

Marc has his head in the clouds. His mother has her feet on the ground. So much so that she manages to get him accepted at a Russian school where, ordinarily, Jews are not allowed to go.
Marc is a mediocre student. He is too much of a dreamer. He does continue to paint, however, even though his parents do not approve.
In fact, he is so obstinate that Feïta-Iga finally gives in and agrees to let him enter the studio of Jehuda Penne, the only painting teacher in Vitebsk.
As soon as he is there, Marc feels reigned in. He knows that he must leave Vitebsk and see more of the world.

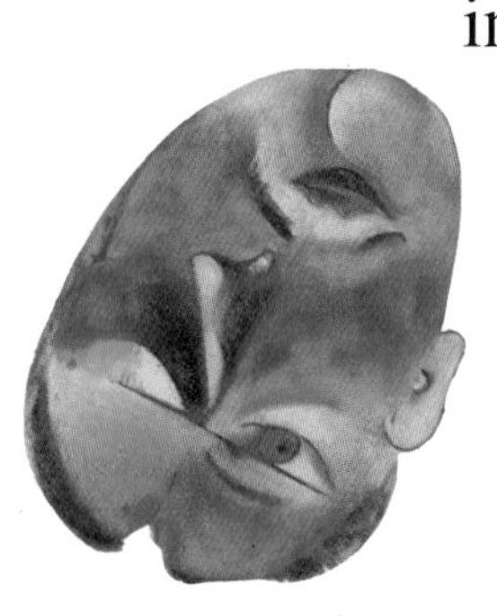

Marc in 1907.

An upside-down poet with a green head. It is not the green cat who would be surprised by him. Marc paints this canvas in Paris in 1911.

Thus he departs, first for St. Petersburg, and then, in 1910, for Paris. Ecstatic, he discovers a new world.

Years later, he will say that he "bit into" Paris with relish.

The young Jewish exile stays close to other painters and poets.

In this shining Parisian galaxy, glimmering with numerous talents, Marc becomes one of its rising stars.

Fiancée

When he leaves Vitebsk for Paris
Marc leaves behind him a
treasure: the young woman whom
he loves.
Her name is Bella. She is
intelligent and beautiful.
Marc stops painting *women* in
order to paint *one woman,* his
beloved, Bella. She is his ideal.
Bella's parents are not
enthusiastic about Marc.
In their family, both the father
and son are jewelers. The idea of
entrusting their daughter to a so-
called artist is not at all pleasing.

1909, *My Fiancée in Black Gloves.*

Memory of a birthday. Bella gives Marc flowers and fabrics for decorating his room.

Between themselves, they say: "What kind of husband will he make, this boy who is as rosy as a girl? He will never manage to earn a living." They are glad to see the intruder leave Russia.
Four years of separation, however, do not change the feelings the young people have for one another. Marc and Bella marry on his return to Vitebsk.

Guerre

War

1914, the year Marc returns to Russia, is for all a dark memory. War breaks out. Marc, who thought to remain in Vitebsk for only several months, is trapped in his own country.
Unable to oppose the murderous deluge, he paints Vitebsk from his window. The wounded who have begun to return recount the horrors of battle.
"The war resounded within me," Marc will say later.
The conflict endures and people grow weak.

1914, *The News Vendor.*
He brings news of the war.

It is too much to bear.
In 1917, Russia is in flames. Revolution convulses the country.
Now everything will change. Marc, who is no longer unknown, is enlisted as the Director of the School of Fine Arts in Vitebsk. He accepts the challenge.
"He chagalles," say his colleagues, laughing, because this word in Russian means, "to take big steps."
He creates a school of painting.
His energy is inexhaustible.

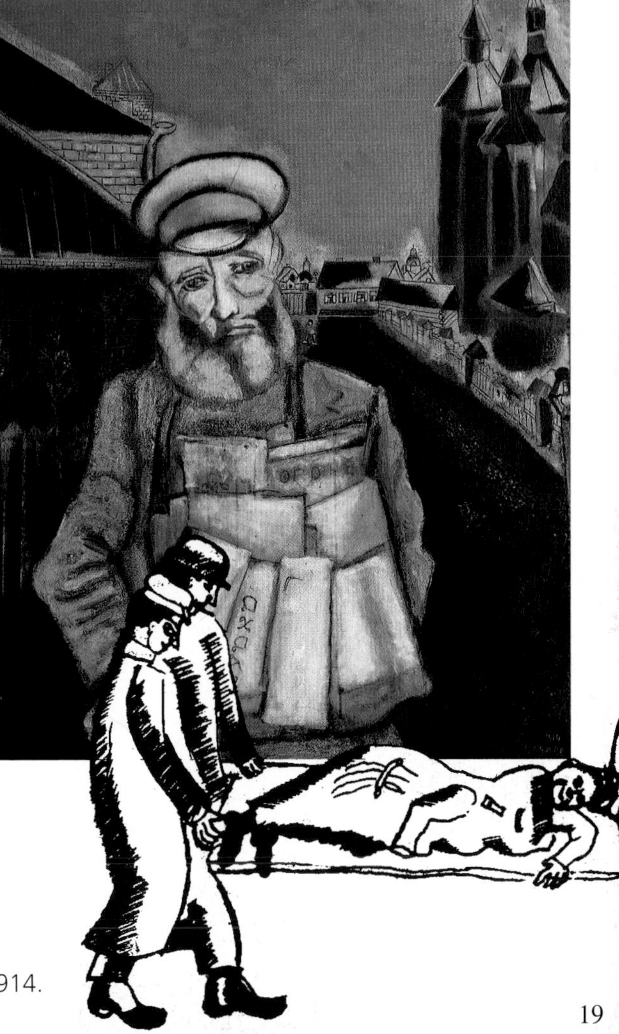

Detail of an ink drawing from 1914.

Holà!

Stop!

Marc believes in the revolution. He brings art into the streets. For the first anniversary of the revolution, he calls on all who are willing to help decorate Vitebsk with large pennants of flying horses, and blue, red, and green cows. As Chagall recounts it: "Throughout the city, my multicolored animals, swollen with revolution, swung in the air."

The directors of the party are perplexed: where are Marx, Lenin and the heroes of the revolution? They begin to distrust this painter who is making the revolution according to his own notions.

They decide it is necessary to put a stop to the activities of this trouble-maker.

Chagall at work.

Here is how, years later, Marc will depict the Russian Revolution—as a ludicrous circus.

Marc is given to understand that they can do without him. Hurt, he takes refuge in Moscow. He is sad. Russia, his Russia, has no need of him.

All he can do is leave.

How painful it is for him to tear himself away from his roots.

Self-Portait from 1914.

Ida

Chagall's Daughter

Baby Ida, sketched by her father in 1917.

"I dreamed of a boy and it was the opposite," confesses Chagall, somewhat ashamed. Ida, the daughter of Marc and Bella, is born in 1916, several months before the start of the revolution. The infancy of Idotchka, which is how she is affectionately called by her father, is marked by the turmoil which shakes Russia.

The family moves from place to place, sometimes even into rooming houses. Life is difficult for them. Caught up in diverse

otchka—her parents' affectionate name for
r—is sick. Bella sits up, sleepless.

political activities, Marc does not paint as often as he would like. He does capture, however, the simple moments of his new family life: Ida's bath, lunch, the minor illnesses.
In the family album, paintings replace photos.
In 1922, when the revolution intensifies, Marc leaves Russia, soon to be joined by Bella and Ida. After a short stay in Berlin, the Chagall family settles in Paris.

Marc, Bella and Ida.

Juif errant

Wandering Jew

Although Marc has left his native land, it remains fully present in his memory.
Like the vagabond who hovers over the roofs of Vitebsk, or the wandering Jew who goes from city to city carrying all his things in only a sack, Marc has stored away the familiar images of his early years. From these, he will recreate the country of his childhood throughout his life.
Recreate and not faithfully reproduce, for he will portray Vitebsk through imagination, as he remembers it. The streets, the cupolas, and the wooden fences of his beloved city take shape under his paintbrush.
A painter-poet, he writes: “The country which I find in my soul is mine alone.

1915–20. *Over Vitebsk.*
The vagabond has put all of his possessions into his sack.

I enter there without a passport as into my own home." Vitebsk will live in him forever.

Kaléidoscope

Kaleidoscope

Chagall is a storyteller who uses colors to tell his stories. Often on a canvas, he juxtaposes successive episodes from the same story.
The painting, *Me and My Village,* makes one think of a kaleidoscope, that magic cylinder in which the play of mirrors creates a multitude of images.
In this painting, bursts of life are organized around a central circle. All mixes together, the past, the present and the make-believe.
Chagall depicts himself at the right with a green face and white lips. Through the play of his eyes with those of a white cow, he makes houses of painted wood, a girl milking a cow, and a man going to reap the meadow appear.
Everything is very strange.

1911–12, *Me and My Village.* Around the central red circle, memories arise in dazzling bursts.

Some of the houses are pitched on their roofs and a woman is upside down. All appears as in a dream.

Lumière liberté

Light, Liberty

In Paris, Marc rediscovers that light which is "more luminous than all sources of artificial light," that "light-liberty" which so seduced him on his first visit.
No longer is he the poor, unknown painter arriving alone at a large Parisian train station.
His work is known, having been exhibited in Germany and Moscow.
He has become famous. His friends—painters and poets—rejoice at his safe return. The rumor had been that he had disappeared in the upheavals of the revolution.
At this time in Paris, there are a number of

Marc, Bella, and Ida
in their Parisian apartment. On the wall, we can see, *The Birthday* and *The Blue House.*

1913, *Paris through the Window.* "Paris is my second Vitebsk," says Marc.

different movements in painting, but Marc declines to take part in any of them.
He is far too independent for that.
He paints as he, Chagall, paints and that is all.

Mariés

Married

In marrying Bella, Marc finds happiness. His paintings do not cease to celebrate the joy of their union with which he is filled. In his skies, the enwrapped newly weds float gently.
Their love makes them light and their happiness enables them to soar above the realities of life.

1917–18, double portrait with Ida and a mauve angel.

The lovers escape the world. Vitebsk, Moscow, Paris, and later New York, Nice and Vence.
The scene changes, but the couple is eternal. Chagall's newlyweds seem fragile, but one should not be fooled. They have overcome wars, conflicts, stupidity and intolerance.
Love gives them wings.

1938, the newlyweds fly over the Eiffel Tower in good company.

Nature

The uprooted Chagall, eternally nostalgic for Vitebsk, has found a new country.
He adopts France. Not only Paris, but the entire country.
With Bella and Ida, he discovers Normandy and Brittany, the Alps and the South.
He is amazed by the diversity of th French landscape. Marc's palette softens. He paints bouquets with th splendor of gardens.
In his paintings, lovers, free from care, whisper solemn oaths to each other.

1924, *Ida at the Window,* on the island of Brehat in Brittany.

Faces arise is the midst of flowers. He invents living still-lifes.
"In France," he will later confess, "I was born for a second time."
In 1937, he obtains French citizenship.

1930, *Pine Cones,* with a miniature Bella under the chair.

1938, *White Crucifixion.* Christ on the cross is dressed in a traditional Jewish prayer shawl.

Ombre

Shadow

At this time, once again, the skies above the world darken. Scarcely twenty years after World War I the Second World War breaks out. Persecutions against the Jews multiply. Chagall, along with a number of other artists, decides to flee to the USA.

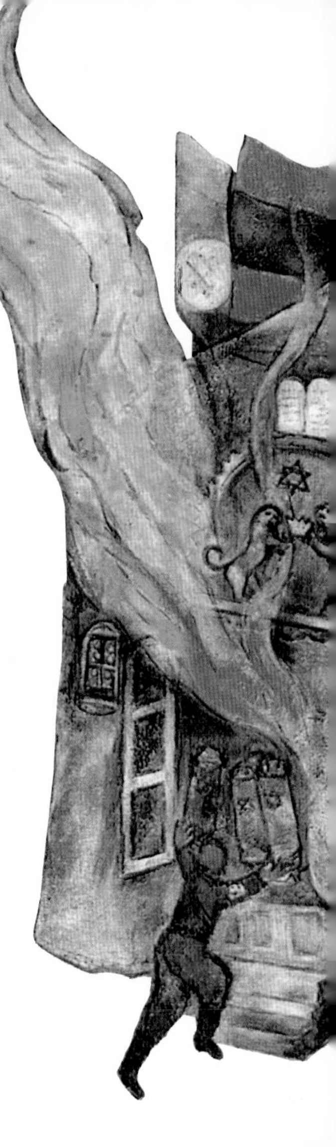

On May 7, 1941, he embarks from Marseille for a new world. He does not speak a word of English, but that is not o serious for he speaks the universal language of painting. Moreover, in the USA, he is already known. He is received with open arms and put to work. Nevertheless, he suffers, for he knows that his fellow Jews are being hunted down and martyred throughout the world. He paints somber canvases which speak of exodus, torture and desolation.

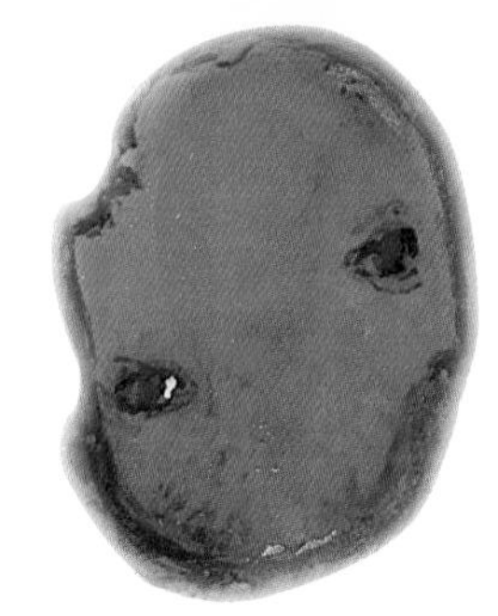

Pile

Heads or Tails

Heads: Happiness
Tails: Unhappiness
Sometimes the two form a pair.
For Chagall, 1944 is a two-sided year. On one side is happiness: Paris is liberated, and his family can finally foresee a return to France. On the other, unhappiness: Bella falls gravely ill and dies three days later. Marc is numb with grief. Throughout many, long months, he cannot work.

A double Biblical face: King David and Bathsheba, his beloved.

et face

He has lost his wife, his muse, his accomplice.
When Marc goes back to work, he portrays people with two heads.
He remembers that life brings both laughter and tears; that dream is the hidden side of reality; and that the past and the future are inseparably linked.

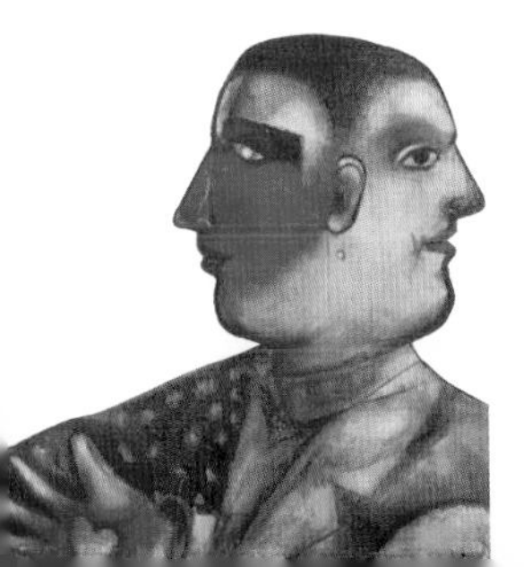

1950, *Mauve Nude with Double Head.*

Quelques

Characters

Marc works on scenery for the Theater of Jewish Art.

Several characters, a stage and some scenery: the theater has always attracted Chagall. In 1920, before leaving Russia, he paints murals and scenery for the Theater of Jewish Art in Moscow.
On the walls, he happily revives the fiddlers and dancer-acrobats who enchanted the holidays throughout his youth.
In this tiny theater, which is soon renamed, "Chagall's box," it is life which sings. In Soviet Russia, however, there is no appreciation for such free-spirited song.

Detail from *Introduction to the Theater of Jewish Art.*

personnages...

Chagall's canvases are rolled up, stashed away and forgotten. In the course of his long life, however, Chagall will have other occasions to work on decoration. In 1964, the French ask him to create a new ceiling for the Paris opera.

Another detail: Marc paints himself in an orange suit in the arms of a director.

Rhapsodie

Rhapsody

While he paints, Marc recalls tunes from the past. On Sabbath days, his Uncle Neuch, the butcher, would grab his violin and break into a wild rhapsody, one of those ageless tunes that make one want to dance.
As his Uncle's bow flew over the strings, the music would rise: whining, lively, and at times strangely melancholic.
The fiddler is one of the key characters in Chagall's paintings. He is the painter's double, a companion spirit. His music protects him from everything.
It is the shell which permits him to escape from

In one of the panels of the Theater of Jewish Art, a fiddler dances, balancing himself on the roofs.

the world. At times, through the music's power, the musician and his instrument become one. Chagall invents the man-violin who, tender and naïve, personifies the spirit of music.

Man-Violin, detail of a lithograph from 1977.

Sur un fil

On a Tightrope

Marc has a passion for the circus.
And since the circus represents all that is marvelous, strange, dream-like and even impossible, this is hardly surprising.
He loves the acrobats and the women on horseback, the tightrope walkers and the jugglers.
Chagall, who moves with grace and lightness along the thread of his memories, is himself a kind of tightrope walker.
At the end of the 1920s, Ambrose Vollard, the famous Parisian art dealer,

1930, *The Acrobat.*

Nestled in the sun, the moon plays the violin.

commissions Chagall to do a painting on the theme of the circus. The painter and the old man pass their evenings together at the Cirque d'Hiver. Marc never forgets his harlequin friends. He will paint them throughout his life.

1950. *The Blue Circus.* A flying fish, a green horse and a trapezist whose hair, even with her head hanging down, remains perfectly in place.

Tendresse

Tenderness

"Your white train floats and flutters in the sky," writes Marc.
The memory of Bella, luminous and fleeting continues to haunt Marc's paintings and poems.
On returning from the United States, he settles in the South of France, at first in Saint-Jean-Cap-Ferrat, then in Vence. There, in the land of sun, he meets Valentine, who

1953–56, *Portrait of Vava.*

Marc and Vava with spade-shaped heads, like the figures on a playing card. Behind them, the village of St. Paul-de-Vence.

is called, Vava. Like him, she is Russian and an exile.
Everything begins again. On July 12, 1952, Marc and Valentina marry.
In the autumn of his life—he is now sixty-five—the tender presence of Vava provides him with the support he needs in order to create.
She will care devotedly for him for more than thirty years.

Marc with Vava in his studio in 1952.

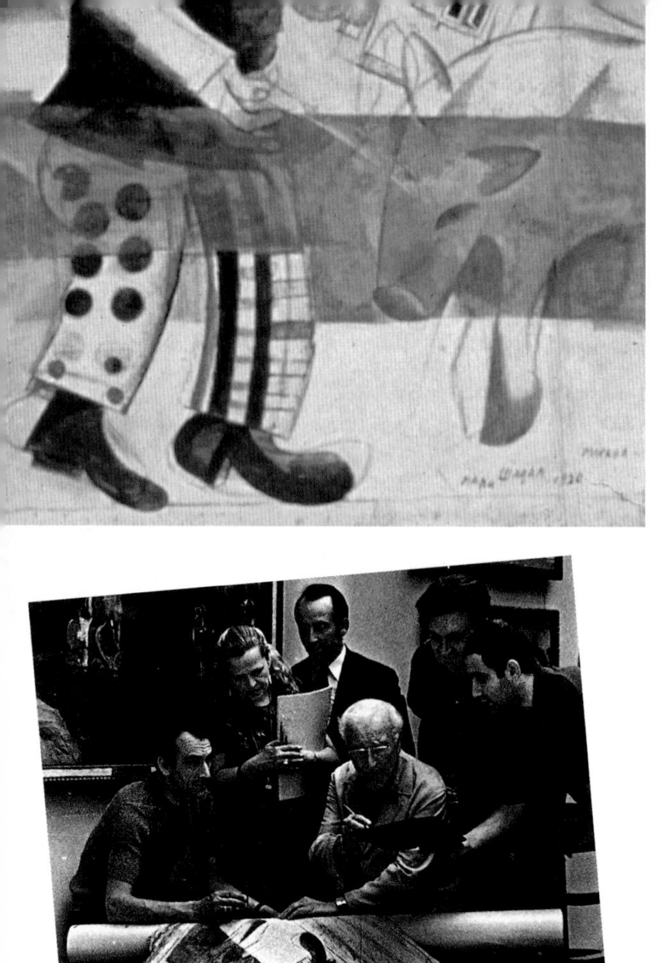

U.R.S.S

U.S.S.R.

In 1973, Marc, now more than 80 years old, travels to the U.S.S.R. accompanied by Vava.
After fifty years of absence, he finds his country greatly changed by revolution.
The Soviet Union is very different from the Russia of the past.
Chagall is happy to see Moscow and the canvases of the Theater of Jewish Art, which he had thought lost.
It fills him with great emotion to be able to put the signature of a now famous painter onto the immense paintings of his youth. He does not have any interest in returning to Vitebsk, however.

1975-76, *The Prodigal Son*, with Vitebsk as the backdrop.

All those whom he loved have disappeared. He prefers his memories to a sad reality.

When he returns to France, he paints *The Prodigal Son.* This painting expresses his sentiments better than words ever could.

Marc rediscovers his country as a child rediscovers his father after a long absence.

He is received with open arms.

Vert

Green

1914, Marc.

1920, the fiddler.

1966, Vava.

Since the beginning, almost ritually, Chagall
has painted the faces of his people green.
Green, the old Jew and the fiddler.
Green, the painter and the face of Vava.
Green, the lovers tenderly entwined.
They are not green with fear, cold, or rage.
Green, it is said, is the color of hope.
For Chagall, it is perhaps more than that.
It is a sign of gratitude, the magic color of
fantasy and freedom.

1914–15, *The Lovers.*

cloWn

Red, yellow, and blue, the clown is a burst of color. He only has to appear for there to be laughter. Like the painter or the fiddler, he is a great artist, at once an acrobat, a musician and a philosopher.

1969, detail from the lithograph,
The Magician of Paris.

It is a long time since Marc has painted this brother of dream and of the marvelous, whose grimaces and pranks conceal much work and sometimes even tears.
Marc knows that the clown is the indispensable fool who is able to turn the grayness of life into great bursts of laughter.
Under his brush, the clown is rarely grotesque.
More often, he is moving.
Chagall's clowns have the grace of poets.

X

X as in
crossroads.
Chagall builds a world at the
crossing of life's paths: those of
childhood, exile, love and death.
At this crossroads, Chagall's
world is unlike any other.
His world spins quickly, to the
point where one becomes giddy.
At that moment, everything
becomes possible.

ish with wings of fire traverse the
ky, flapping their arms; the moon
onsoles itself by playing the
iolin; chickens take on dancer's
odies; clocks glide through the air
hile beating time; sheep piously
arry candlesticks for the Jewish
olidays; the Eiffel Tower watches
ver the *isbas* of a modest Jewish
eighborhood.
t the crossing of paths, all is
ixed together into
great song of
fe.

The Marionettist. Like him, the painter is master of his creatures.

1950, *The Joy of Life.*
All the faces have
almond-shaped eyes.

Yeux

Eyes

Eyes—eloquent, elongated,
almond-shaped.
"Eyes like none other in the world," remarks Bella when she meets Marc for the first time. Eyes like "small boats which appear in the distance."
If one observes well, it can be seen that most of Chagall's creatures have inherited the shape of his eyes.
Only the look changes.

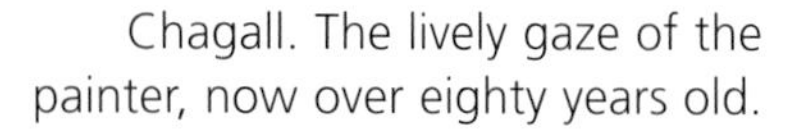

Chagall. The lively gaze of the painter, now over eighty years old.

Chagall's is piercing, lively, freely mocking.
That of his creatures is irresistibly tender beneath their eyelids hemmed with blue or black.
With tilted head, the curly-maned horse looks out with gentle eyes.
The rooster, whose feathers look like a bouquet, has an attentive gaze.
Another sentimental story.

Self-Portrait from 1924–25.

Zone

Sacred Space

Chagall does not practice religion as his parents did. He has retained, however, a strong sense of the sacred.
When he is asked in the 1930s to illustrate the Bible, he undertakes this work with passion.
He goes to the Holy Land, and he explores the techniques of mosaic and stained glass, which are new to him.
Nothing is too grand for celebrating the Book of Books.

1931, *Noah Releasing the Dove.*

sacrée

1973, in the hills of Nice, ıagall inaugurates his useum of the Biblical essage.

is message can be summed in three words: peace, otherhood and love.

ɔve of others and a emendous love of life.

hen Chagall dies on arch 28, 1985, he is almost)0 years old. He has ceased to ıg and dance the century in inting.

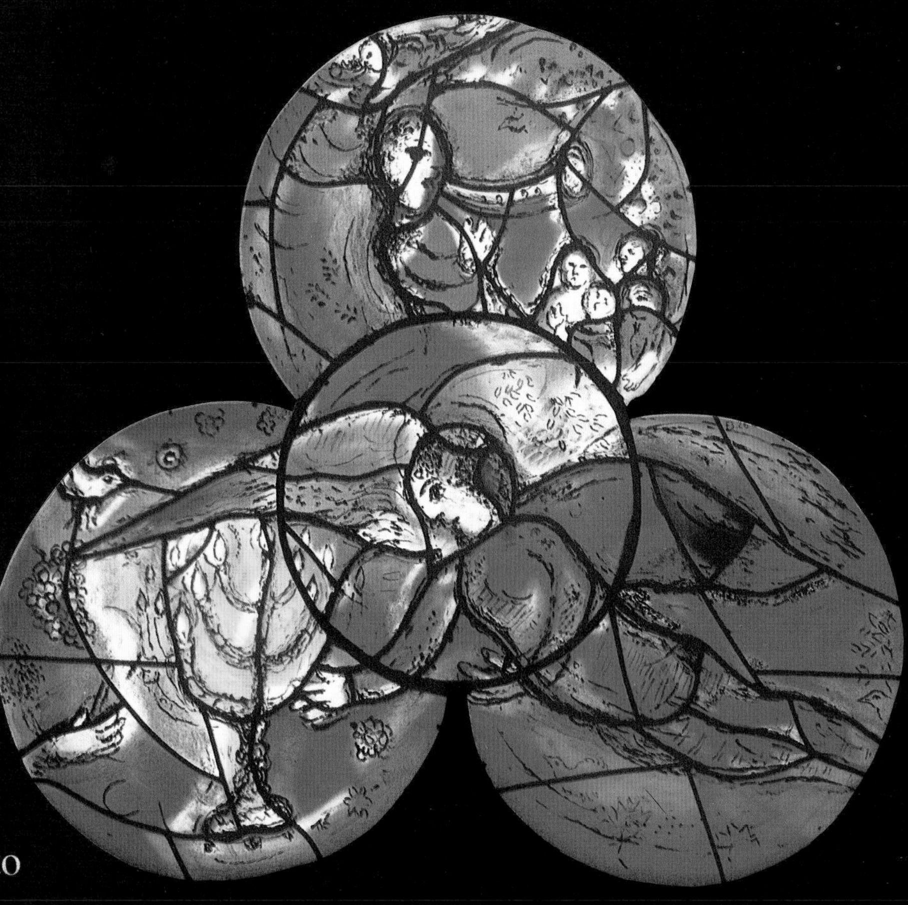

An angel passes—a detail of a stained glass window of the cathedral St. Stephen, in Mayence, Germany.

List of Illustrations

Eiffel Tour, painting, 1938-39, Musée national d'art moderne, Centre G. Pompidou, Paris.

Pages 32-33: *Pine Cones,* painting, 1930, Peyra-Cava series, private collection. *Bouquet in the Window,* drawing, Archives of Ida Chagall. *Ida at the Window,* painting, 1924, Stedelijk Museum, Amsterdam.

Pages 34-35: *White Crucifixion,* painting, 1938, The Art Institute, Chicago.

Pages 36-37: *David and Bathsheba,* lithogaph, 1956, Musée National du Message Biblique Marc Chagall, Nice. *The Dream of Lamon and Dryas,* lithograph (detail), 1958-61, private collection. *Paris through the Window* (detail). *Mauve Nude with Double Head,* painting, 1950, private collection, Basel.

Pages 38-39: Chagall painting, photograph, 1920, Archives of Ida Chagall. *Introduction to the Theater of Jewish Art* (details).

Pages 40-41: *Music,* Theater of Jewish Art, painting, 1920, private collection. *The Musician,* engraving, private collection. Artists, lithograph (detail), 1977, private collection.

Pages 42-43: *Clown-Trapezist,* ink drawing, private collection. *The Acrobat,* painting, 1930, Musée national d'art moderne, Centre G. Pompidou, Paris. *Blue Circus,* Musée national d'art moderne, Centre G. Pompidou, Paris.

Pages 44-45: *Portrait of Vava,* painting, 1953-56, private collection. Photo Patrick Gérin. Chagall and Vava in his studio. photograph, 1952, Archives of Ida Chagall. *Happiness,* lithograph, 1969, private collection.

Pages 46-47: *Introduction to the Theater of Jewish Art* (detail). *Self-Portrait,* engraving, illustration for *My Life. The Prodigal Son,* painting, 1975-76, Paris, estate of Ida Chagall.

Pages 48-49: *Self-Portrait in Green,* 1914, Musée national d'art moderne, Centre G. Pompidou, Paris. Photo Philippe Migeat. *Music* (detail). *Portrait of Vava,* painting (detail), 1966, private collection. Photo P. Gérin. *Introduction to the Theater of Jewish Art* (detail). *Lovers in Green,* painting (detail), 1914-15, D.G. Efros, Moscow.

Pages 50-51: *Circus Under Stars,* lithograph (detail), 1965, private collection.*The Clown,* lithograph (detail), 1962-67, private collection. *Circus Rider on a Winged Horse,* lithograph (detail), 1956, private collection. *The Magician of Paris,* lithograph (detail), 1969, private collection.

Pages 52-53: *Time is a River without Banks,* painting, 1930-39, Museum of Modern Art, New York. *The Painter with His Easel,* ink drawing, 1914, Musée national d'art moderne, Centre G. Pompidou, Paris. Photo Philippe Migeat. *The Marionettist,* ink drawing, 1916, Musée national d'art moderne, Centre G. Pompidou, Paris. Photo Philippe Migeat. *The Juggler,* painting, 1943, The Art Institute, Chicago.

Pages 54-55: *The Joy of Life,* painting, 1950, private collection. Chagall, photograph, private collection. *Self-Portrait,* ink drawing, Musée national d'art moderne, Centre G. Pompidou, Paris. *Flowering Feathers,* painting, 1942, Musée national d'art moderne, Centre G. Pompidou, Paris.

Pages 56-57: *Noah Releasing the Dove,* gouache, 1931, Musée national du Message Biblique Marc Chagall. Stained glass (detail), Mayence, Saint Stephen Cathedral, Kunstverlag Maria Laach.